D1123978

SPENDING & SAVING MONEY

By Steffi Cavell-Clarke

CRABTREE
PUBLISHING COMPANY
WWW.CRABTREEBOOKS.COM

Published in Canada
Crabtree Publishing
616 Welland Avenue
St. Catharines, ON
L2M 5V6

Published in the United States
Crabtree Publishing
PMB 59051
350 Fifth Ave, 59th Floor
New York, NY 10118

Published by Crabtree Publishing Company in 2019

All rights reserved. No part of this publication may be reproduced, stored in a retrieval system or be transmitted in any form or by any means, electronic, mechanical, photocopying, recording, or otherwise, without the prior written permission of the copyright owner.

©2018 BookLife Publishing

Author: Steffi Cavell-Clarke

Editors: Kirsty Holmes, Janine Deschenes

Design: Jasmine Pointer

Proofreader: Melissa Boyce

**Production coordinator and
prepress technician (interior):** Margaret Amy Salter

Prepress technician (covers): Ken Wright

Print coordinator: Katherine Berti

Photographs

Shutterstock: ©Vladimir Sazonov p 10 (coins); ©Seika Chujo p 11

All images from Shutterstock

Printed in the U.S.A./122018/CG20181005

Library and Archives Canada Cataloguing in Publication

Cavell-Clarke, Steffi, author
    Spending and saving money / Steffi Cavell-Clarke.

(Our values)
Includes index.
Issued in print and electronic formats.
ISBN 978-0-7787-5432-9 (hardcover).--
ISBN 978-0-7787-5495-4 (softcover).--ISBN 978-1-4271-2223-0 (HTML)

    1. Children--Finance, Personal--Juvenile literature. 2. Finance, Personal--Juvenile literature. 3. Saving and investment--Juvenile literature. I. Title.

HG179.C384 2018   j332.024   C2018-905495-6
                                       C2018-903496-4

Library of Congress Cataloging-in-Publication Data

Names: Cavell-Clarke, Steffi, author.
Title: Spending and saving money / Steffi Cavell-Clarke.
Description: New York : Crabtree Publishing Company, [2018] |
  Series: Our values | Includes index.
Identifiers: LCCN 2018043790 (print) | LCCN 2018045426 (ebook) |
  ISBN 9781427122230 (Electronic) |
  ISBN 9780778754329 (hardcover) |
  ISBN 9780778754954 (pbk.)
Subjects: LCSH: Money--Juvenile literature. | Saving and investment--Juvenile
  literature. | Income--Juvenile literature.
Classification: LCC HG221.5 (ebook) | LCC HG221.5 .C349 2018 (print) |
  DDC 332.024--dc23
LC record available at https://lccn.loc.gov/2018043790

CONTENTS

Words that look like **this** can be found in the glossary on page 24.

WHAT ARE VALUES?

Values are the things that you believe are important, such as trying your hardest at school and **respecting** others. They are the ideas and beliefs that help us to work and live together peacefully in a community.

Helping others

Sharing your ideas

Respecting others

Values make our communities better places to live. Think about the values in your community. What is important to you and the people around you?

Working hard at school

Making your own choices

Spending money responsibly

NEEDS AND WANTS

We have needs and wants. Our needs are the things we need to survive, such as food, water, clothing, and shelter. Our wants are things that we would like to have. They might include a chocolate bar, a new pair of sunglasses, or the latest video game.

We need money to buy the things we want and need. Our wants and needs are met by goods and services. Goods are things such as fruits and shoes.

Services are the things people do for us. Doctors examine us and help keep us healthy. Mechanics fix our vehicles, and teachers help us learn new things.

WHY IS MONEY IMPORTANT?

People **exchange** money to buy the goods and services that help them meet their wants and needs. If you need food and clothes or want toys, you need money to pay for them. We need money to pay for homes that give us shelter, and heat to keep our homes warm.

People work to earn money to buy goods and services. To earn money, people make goods and provide services. They are called **producers**. When we buy goods and services, we are called **consumers**.

MONEY EVERYWHERE

Money is used all around the world. Different countries have different money. This is called their **currency**. Have you ever seen money from another country?

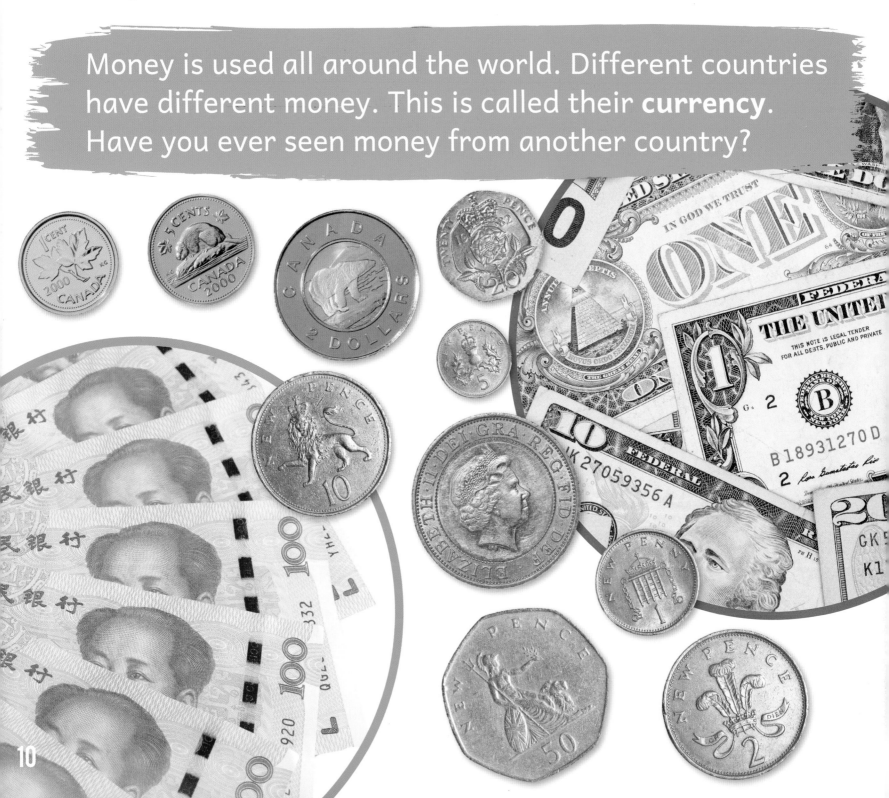

It is very important that we keep our money safe. We can keep our money in a purse or a wallet so it is easy to carry around with us without losing it. Many people keep their money in a **bank account**. Banks hold a lot of money and keep it safe.

11

EARNING MONEY

Earning money is the way we get the goods and services we want and need. Adults earn money by having a job. Maria's parents both work. Her mother works as an **accountant**, and her stepfather works as a teacher.

Both of Maria's parents are producers. They provide services in exchange for money.

Children can earn money too! Joshua's parents give him an **allowance** for doing jobs around the house. Joshua has to choose between spending his allowance on small things, or saving it up for something that costs more money. Making choices about how you spend and save your money is called **budgeting**.

WHAT IS A BUDGET?

A budget is a plan for how money earned will be spent. Budgets help us spend our money responsibly. They make sure that all needs are met before any wants are bought. A budget makes sure that the money coming in is enough to meet all of a person's needs—and some of their wants.

Lily is saving up to buy a new sweatshirt. She made a budget to show how much of her weekly allowance she will save until she can buy the sweatshirt. Lily also loves ice cream! She makes sure she sets aside $5 every month so that she can buy a tasty treat after school. Lily's budget helps her reach her goals and enjoy a treat once in a while.

SETTING GOALS

Making a budget starts with setting goals for how we want to spend our money. Short-term goals are things we can buy right away. Medium-term goals might take a few weeks or months of saving. Long-term goals take many months, or even years, of saving.

A short-term goal might be groceries needed for dinner that evening.

A medium-term goal might be to buy a new pair of shoes or the latest toy or video game.

A long-term goal is something like a new car, house, or a big family vacation.

SAVING MONEY

Saving money is an important part of making a budget. It is what allows us to afford the medium- and long-term goals we cannot buy right away. We can put the money we save in a safe place and add to it over time.

A safe place for a small amount of money might be a piggy bank. A safe place for bigger amounts of money is a bank account.

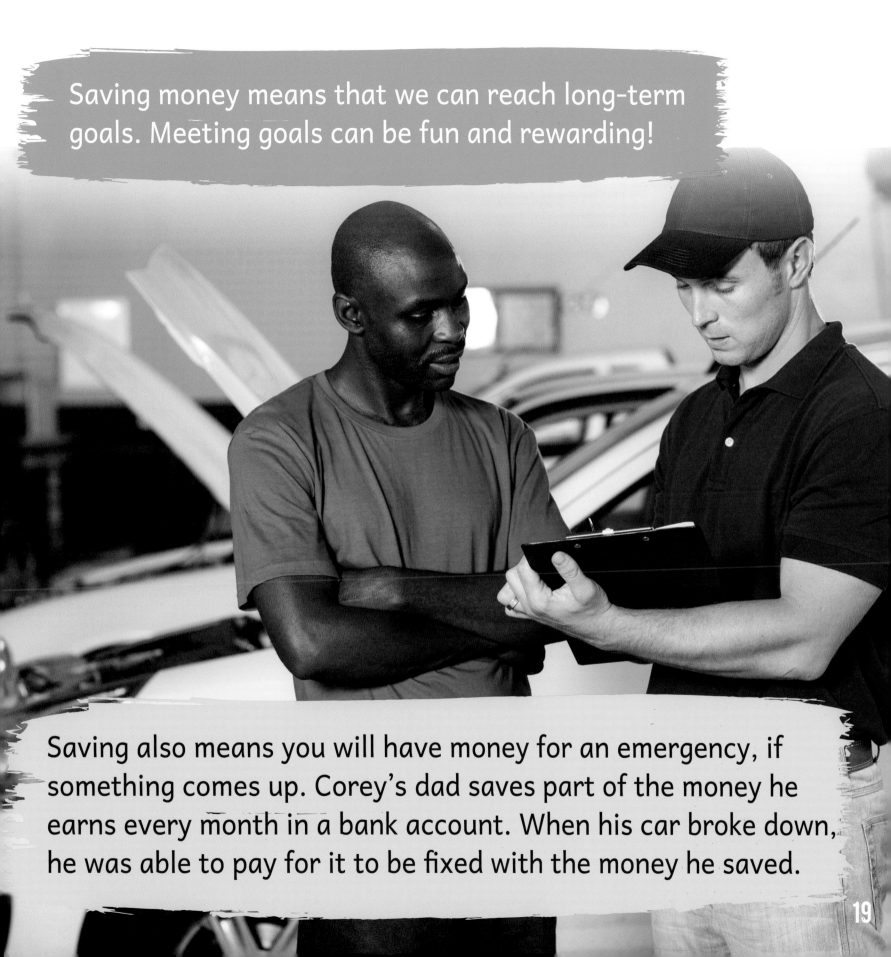

Saving money means that we can reach long-term goals. Meeting goals can be fun and rewarding!

Saving also means you will have money for an emergency, if something comes up. Corey's dad saves part of the money he earns every month in a bank account. When his car broke down, he was able to pay for it to be fixed with the money he saved.

RAISING MONEY

Money can be used to help people rather than to buy things for our own wants and needs. Many people do not have the money they need to buy goods and services to meet their needs. They may rely on help from others to be able to do so.

There are many **charities** that raise money for good causes, such as helping people who have difficulty providing for their family's needs. People might **donate** to charities so that they can help others meet their needs.

Food Donations

Charities might help people in your local community or in the global community.

MAKING A DIFFERENCE

To contribute to charities, we could donate clothes and take food to food banks. We could donate unused goods, such as toys, to stores run by charities. At these stores, people can buy goods at lower prices. We can also donate money to charities or raise money for causes we care about.

Learning about good ways to spend and save money is an important skill. You can start by creating a budget of your own. Write down all of the ways that you earn money right now. Then, write down your goals. How can you meet your goals with the money you earn? Don't forget to save for things you can't buy right away.

Is donating to a charity one of your goals?

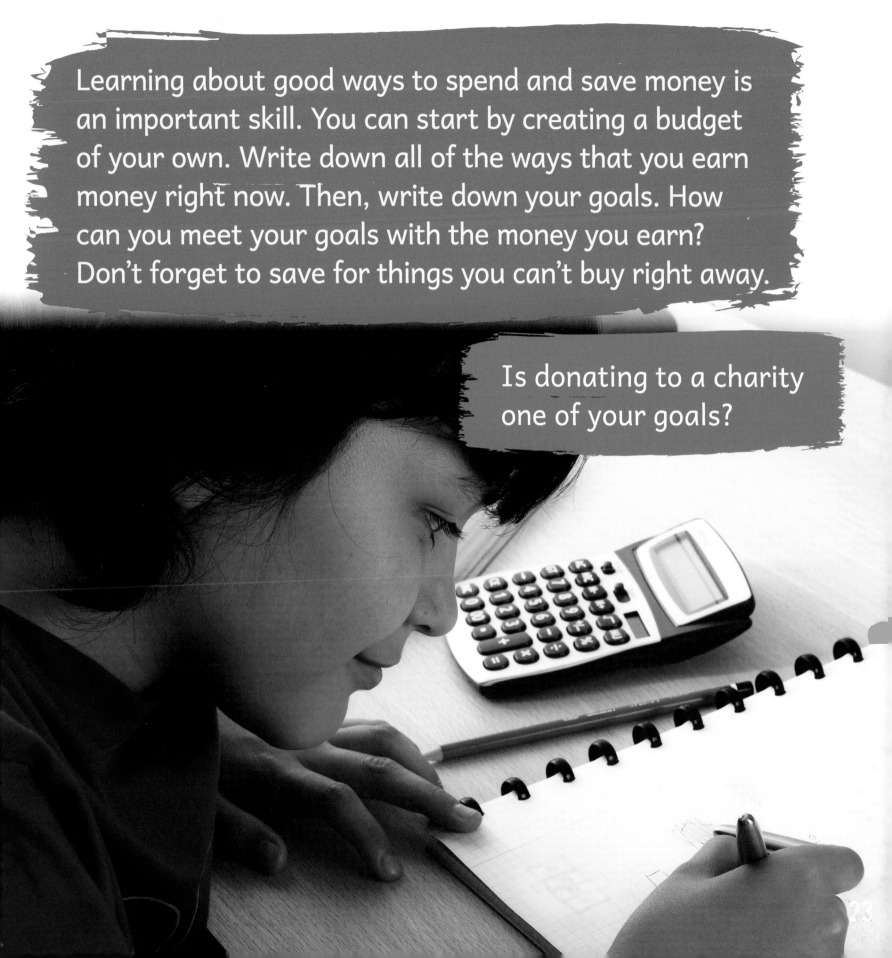

GLOSSARY

accountant [*uh*-KOUN-tnt] A person whose job it is to inspect how a person or business's money is earned and spent

allowance [*uh*-LOU-*uh*ns] An amount of money given regularly

bank account [bangk *uh*-KOUNT] An agreement with a bank in which a person can put money in and take it out

budgeting [BUHJ-it-ing] Planning how money earned will be spent

charities [CHAR-i-tees] Organizations that help and raise money for those in need

consumers [k*uh*n-SOO-mers] People who buy goods and services

currency [KUR-*uh*n-see] The money used in a certain country

donate [DOH-neyt] Giving away something, such as money or clothing

exchange [iks-CHEYNJ] Trade

producers [pr*uh*-DOO-sers] People who make goods and provide services

respecting [ri-SPEK-ting] Giving someone or something the care or attention it deserves

responsibly [ri-SPON-s*uh*-blee] Doing something in a dependable and trustworthy way

INDEX